Saving a Species

Angela Davids

✳ Smithsonian

© 2019 Smithsonian Institution. The name "Smithsonian" and the Smithsonian logo are registered trademarks owned by the Smithsonian Institution.

Contributing Author

Allison Duarte

Consultants

Michael Brown-Palsgrove
Curator
Smithsonian's National Zoo

Laurie Thompson
Assistant Curator
Smithsonian's National Zoo

Jen Zoon
Communications Specialist
Smithsonian's National Zoo

Stephanie Anastasopoulos, M.Ed.
TOSA, STREAM Integration
Solana Beach School District

Publishing Credits

Rachelle Cracchiolo, M.S.Ed., *Publisher*
Conni Medina, M.A.Ed., *Managing Editor*
Diana Kenney, M.A.Ed., NBCT, *Content Director*
Véronique Bos, *Creative Director*
Robin Erickson, *Art Director*
Michelle Jovin, M.A., *Associate Editor*
Mindy Duits, *Senior Graphic Designer*
Smithsonian Science Education Center

Image Credits: p.4, pp.6–7, p.8 (top), p.10, p.13 (all), p.14 (bottom, all), p.15, p.19 (top), p.23 (left), p.27 (top), p.32 (right) © Smithsonian; p.5 (top) Giannis Papanikos/ Shutterstock; p.12 (left) courtesy IUCN-SSC Otter Specialist Group; p.17 (top) Mark Moffett/ Minden Pictures/Newscom; p.20 (top) Roberth Harding Productions/Newscom; p.20 (bottom) Roger Allen/Splash News/Newscom; p.21 (top) Manpreet Romana/AFP/ Getty Images; pp.26–27 Douglas Faulkner/Science Source; p.27 (bottom) Dan Guravich/ Science Source; all other images from iStock and/or Shutterstock.

Library of Congress Cataloging-in-Publication Data

Names: Davids, Angela, 1973- author.
Title: Saving a species / Angela Davids.
Description: Huntington Beach, CA : Teacher Created Materials, Inc., [2019] |
   Audience: Grade 4 to 6. | Includes index. |
Identifiers: LCCN 2018018099 (print) | LCCN 2018020182 (ebook) | ISBN
   9781493869466 (E-book) | ISBN 9781493867066 (paperback)
Subjects: LCSH: Endangered species--Conservation--Juvenile literature.
Classification: LCC QL83 (ebook) | LCC QL83 .D38 2019 (print) | DDC
   591.68--dc23
LC record available at https://lccn.loc.gov/2018018099

Smithsonian

© 2019 Smithsonian Institution. The name "Smithsonian"
and the Smithsonian logo are registered trademarks
owned by the Smithsonian Institution.

Teacher Created Materials

5301 Oceanus Drive
Huntington Beach, CA 92649-1030
www.tcmpub.com
ISBN 978-1-4938-6706-6

© 2019 Teacher Created Materials, Inc.

Table of Contents

Animals at Risk

Over 1,500 animals live at Smithsonian's National Zoo and Conservation Biology Institute in Washington, DC. Each one has its own story. But the five zoo animals in this book fight the same challenge: **extinction**. Why is that? Farmers and villagers take over their land. Humans destroy fragile environments when they clear forests and overfish. **Poachers** sell animals for food and fur to make a living. It seems that people are their worst enemies.

But people can also be heroes. They can save animals. **Conservationists** protect plants, water, and animals. They learn about the problem and take part in the solution. Researchers travel into the wild to study animals where they live. **Zoologists** work behind the scenes at zoos. They gather information about animal health and behavior. These are the people with a passion for saving **species**!

Now, let's meet Tusa, Chowder, Bei Bei, Niko, and Lek. They have all lived at the Asia Trail exhibit at Smithsonian's National Zoo. Learn about where they are from, what they eat, and why they are in danger. Then, see what people are doing to save them. Let the adventure begin!

An animal keeper feeds a red panda a grape.

A hippo swims in an aquarium.

Beauty and Function

People who plan exhibits are known as habitat designers. They re-create natural environments for animals in a zoo. Exhibits also need to look nice to attract visitors. Imagine a cool and misty waterfall. Can you picture lush, green plants? And how do you feel when you see an aquarium with soothing blue lights? The ideal zoo exhibit appeals to animals and people.

Tusa the Red Panda

First thing's first: red pandas are not the same as giant pandas. They aren't even bears. If you ever met Tusa at the National Zoo, you would say he looked more like a raccoon. The word *ponya* is used in the country Nepal to describe an animal that eats bamboo. People believe *panda* comes from this word. Amazingly, red panda fossils from five million years ago have been found in North America. At some point, these animals disappeared from that continent and today are found only in Asia. They live in China, India, Myanmar, Tibet, and Nepal.

A Disappearing Act

Red pandas thrive in habitats with large forests near water. They climb high into trees to relax and get warm in the sun. They can hide from predators there. Red pandas eat mostly bamboo, so they need land with plenty of these plants.

This species is **endangered** because its habitat is disappearing. Humans clear the forests where they live to make room for farming. They chop down trees for firewood or to sell as lumber. People also kill red pandas to eat them and sell their fur. With all of these challenges, there may be fewer than 2,500 adult red pandas left in the wild.

Map Key
area where red pandas live and travel

Species may be endangered if there are not a lot of those animals left in the wild or if their habitats are threatened. Another reason is if they live only in a few places.

Tusa

This red panda cub was born at Smithsonian's Conservation Biology Institute in 2017.

A zoologist feeds a red panda a biscuit for leaf-eaters.

Bamboo Buffet

Tusa and his **mate**, Asa, lived together in Smithsonian's National Zoo. Zoologists worked hard to make sure Tusa and Asa stayed healthy and ate well. Animal keepers fed them grapes and apples, plus special biscuits for leaf-eating animals. In the wild, red pandas eat 1 to 2 kilograms (2.2 to 4.4 pounds) of bamboo leaves each day. At the Zoo, they snacked on bamboo all the time. Bamboo doesn't provide red pandas with much energy though, so they slept about half the day.

People Taking Action

Many laws try to protect red pandas. But people still hunt them. And they still cut down bamboo forests. A clever way to defend red pandas is the Forest Guardians program. The Red Panda Network organizes this program and collects donations. They raise money for each person who becomes a Forest Guardian. These guardians get to know people in their communities. They earn their respect. They even become friends. When they talk to people about how to save red pandas from extinction, it changes their behavior. This can be more powerful than any law.

SCIENCE

Let's Just Chill

When weather gets cold, red pandas use less energy. They become **dormant**, which means their body functions slow and they use fewer **calories**. This lowers the amount of heat that escapes from their bodies. They also roll into balls, which helps hold in the heat. Every few hours, they use just enough energy to look for food.

An Otter Named Chowder

Chowder is an Asian small-clawed otter at Smithsonian's National Zoo. He and his mate, Clementine, had nine adorable otter pups. The girls are Pickles, Saffron, Olive, Peaches, Radish, and Rutabaga. The boys are Pork Chop, Turnip, and…Kevin. Zoos around the world are trying to **breed** otters to protect them from extinction. It isn't always easy. So, Chowder's growing family is seen as a great success.

Small-clawed otters are a **vulnerable** species. That means they could become endangered if people don't take action. Researchers are not sure how many are left in the wild. What they do know for sure is that this otter's habitat is shrinking.

An otter's perfect home is a muddy burrow along the water. Streams, marshes, and rice paddies provide otters with plenty of crabs and fish to eat. People are moving closer to these areas, and they compete for the same food as otters. Plus, people remove plants and trees to make room for crops. Then, chemicals used to kill insects pollute the water.

Chowder and his family

An Asian small-clawed otter eats a fish.

Asian small-clawed otters use their very strong teeth to crush the shells of their food. They also leave shellfish they catch out in the sun and wait for their shells to crack open from heat.

On the Move

Otters need energy to swim and play. They burn calories quickly, so they eat often. Shellfish, such as clams, are their favorite. Insects, rodents, and snakes are on the menu too. At the Zoo, otters eat packaged foods, similar to what cats and dogs eat. Animal keepers also put crabs, crickets, and live goldfish around the exhibit for otters to find. The search for food keeps them amused and active, just as it does in the wild.

People Taking Action

Many people think otters are adorable. Could that be what saves them? It's possible. More than 40 years ago, a group of zoologists formed an organization to protect otters. Now, they are using social media and science to meet their goal. Online, you can see why people can't help but share the photos and videos that the IUCN-SSC Otter Specialist Group posts. Because of their work, people want to know more about otters. It's a chance to teach people why otters are at risk and show them what they can do to help. The group shares information about events, petitions, and volunteering. They make it easy to make a difference.

Otter Specialist Group

An animal keeper feeds fish to an otter while an X-ray is taken.

An Asian small-clawed otter tries to get food out of a puzzle feeder made from PVC pipes.

ENGINEERING

Naturally Fun

Animal keepers make simple changes to common items to inspire natural behaviors. In the wild, an otter uses its claws to grab crabs in shallow water. At the Zoo, they dig their claws into PVC pipes with drilled holes for bits of fish.

Introducing Bei Bei

Zoologists celebrated when Bei Bei was born in 2015 at Smithsonian's National Zoo. The Zoo started its panda program in 1972, but Bei Bei is one of only three panda cubs to survive. Mei Xiang (may SHONG) is the mother of all three cubs. She came to the zoo in 2000 from a Chinese conservation program. They hoped she would have many cubs. But there's a big challenge. Female giant pandas want to mate for only a few days each year. That gives pandas a lot less time to breed than other animals. That's one reason there are fewer than 1,900 giant pandas in the wild.

When Bei Bei was born, he weighed about the same as a deck of cards and was smaller than a stapler. Like other pandas, Bei Bei mainly eats bamboo. Adult pandas eat 22 to 36 kg (50 to 80 lb.) of bamboo daily! But they don't have the type of **gut bacteria** needed to digest plants well. That means they get few nutrients from plants and must eat a lot. Giant pandas have also **evolved** to eat a small amount of meat. But that only accounts for about one percent of their daily diet.

Bei Bei and Mei Xiang

three-month-old Bei Bei

In 2016, the organization that tracks at-risk animals removed the giant panda from its endangered species list. That is good news, but the giant panda is still listed as a vulnerable species.

Bei Bei

Threatened Habitat

For millions of years, giant pandas lived in **lowland** forests throughout central China. Now, they live mostly in mountain forests, in only three regions. The forests are separated by crops, highways, and structures. This cuts off populations of pandas from one another. They might reject the few potential mates they meet. Or they might mate with a panda that is related to them. This can negatively affect the health of giant pandas.

People Taking Action

Some scientists describe the separate areas where pandas live as "islands." They are surrounded by damaged habitats. Researchers from Smithsonian's Conservation Biology Institute and Zoo are leading a project to connect these islands. Their idea is to create paths of new forest that will lead from one wildlife preserve to another. They plan to create what they call "corridors." Corridors are like hallways that guide pandas from one place to the next.

Another innovation is the Grain for Green program. In this program, the Chinese government pays farmers to replace their crops with trees. And it is working! China is gaining forestland in some areas. These are small spaces of success, but they offer some hope. Paths of new plants and trees could connect panda groups again. They could also provide the food they need to survive.

Map Key

area where giant pandas live and travel

Workers in China plant spruce trees to grow the forestland.

MATHEMATICS

Sleeping Giants

Researchers have an unusual way of telling how long a giant panda has been napping. Pandas continue to make droppings as they sleep. They make 5 to 10 droppings in two hours. They will have around twice as many in four hours. That's the strange way we know that the typical panda nap can last from two to six hours.

sleeping giant panda

Saving Niko

Niko came to Smithsonian's National Zoo when he was two years old. Researchers delighted at the chance to study a sloth bear up close. Wild sloth bears are difficult to observe. They like to be alone and will attack humans if threatened. Mother bears might even kill their cubs if the cubs aren't healthy. Zoologists around the world try to save this species by learning how it behaves, what makes it sick, and what it needs to eat.

Niko and his female sloth bear friend, Remi, eat a dry food made for **omnivores**, plus fruit and vegetables. They have several meals throughout the day. To keep the bears active and engaged during the day, animal keepers give the bears some of their favorite foods, such as mealworms, crickets, and honey. Sloth bears in the wild mostly eat termites and ants. They sometimes eat **carcasses** that have been left by other predators. When fruit is in season, sloth bears eat mangos and figs, but they cannot digest fruit seeds. Those undigested seeds in the bear's droppings are spread around the forest and become new trees.

Many sloth bears live safely in more than 150 national parks and sanctuaries, but they are still in danger. Fewer than 20,000 sloth bears are left, mostly in Southeast Asia.

Map Key

area where sloth bears live and travel

Niko plays with a puzzle feeder.

6-month-old sloth bear

A Fight for Their Lives

A Kalandar tribesman pulls on a dancing bear's rope.

In the wild, poachers hunt sloth bears to collect a digestive fluid called **bile**. Some people mistakenly believe their bile can cure many diseases. A container of bile the size of a paint can may sell for up to $2 million.

Another threat is the tradition of capturing cubs to use as "dancing bears." For over four hundred years, people have earned money by entertaining tourists with bears. Kalandar tribesmen in India insert a permanent metal ring into a bear's muzzle. They attach a rope to the ring. Then, they pull the rope to make the bear "dance" from pain.

Lily the dancing bear was once blind but had her eyesight restored by Wildlife SOS.

Wildlife SOS co-founder Kartick Satyanarayan hugs a sloth bear he saved from becoming a dancing bear.

People Taking Action

A group called Wildlife SOS strives to end the custom of dancing bears. The organization interviewed the tribesmen to learn what jobs they would want to do instead. More than 600 men volunteered to give up their bears. Many of these men now work as gem cutters, spice packagers, and welders. Wildlife SOS founded schools as well. They have enrolled more than 1,300 Kalandar children so far. Children learn to read, which creates more job opportunities. In the past, girls did not go to school, but now they attend these new schools. Kids are guiding their parents and grandparents into a new way of life.

camera trap
in a forest

TECHNOLOGY

Say Cheese!

Fishing cats can be hard to see at night. A popular way to study where they travel is to set up cameras in the wild. This is called camera trapping. Researchers put hundreds of cameras in places that fishing cats live. When the cameras detect heat and movement using special sensors, they take pictures. Cameras in Indonesia haven't found any fishing cats, which is a cause of concern for researchers.

Meet Lek

Lek lives at Smithsonian's National Zoo. There are not many fishing cats in zoos around the world. The zoos that *do* have fishing cats collaborate to share what they learn. This is critical for the fishing cat species to survive. Because these stealthy animals roam after dark, they are extremely difficult to find and study in nature. It makes it a true challenge for researchers to observe how they act and how they choose mates. Zoologists eagerly hope that Lek will provide some answers.

You can probably guess what Lek's wild relatives like to eat most. They use their long claws to scoop fish and shellfish out of rivers and marshes. Because they love to hunt, they also trap and eat small mammals, birds, and amphibians. In the wild, they drop their food into water and then grab it again. Lek does that in the Zoo too! Lek eats fish, dry cat food, and ground meat made for zoo **carnivores**.

A fishing cat waits for a fish to swim by.

Lek

The Most Dangerous Predator

People are the biggest threat to fishing cats. Almost all the large **wetlands** of Southeast Asia are at risk. People pollute the water with trash and chemicals. Other people take over large sections of water so they can catch fish and shrimp to sell. On land, villagers destroy habitats when they chop down trees to start farms and build cities. Another risk is hunters who sell cats for fur and food. Wildlife experts don't know how many fishing cats live in the wild. They are rarely seen.

People Taking Action

Many people work to study animals in zoos and in nature. A conservationist in Sri Lanka's largest city had a new idea. What about studying fishing cats who live in cities? How do they adapt when much of their habitat is destroyed? She founded the Urban Fishing Cat Conservation Project. Her team discovered fishing cats that live in abandoned houses. They steal fish from garden ponds for food. Now, citizens can report sightings on the group's website. Researchers then set up camera traps in those areas. They safely trap the cats to fit them with GPS collars. Those collars record how far fishing cats travel to return to the wetlands that surround the city. Scientists use that to learn how they adjust to city life.

A fishing cat walks along a tree branch.

A worker uses a tractor to clear part of Borneo Rainforest in Southeast Asia.

Fishing cats can swim! Their long, round heads are good for diving underwater to grab fish with their teeth. Their fur is water-resistant to keep them dry.

25

How You Can Save a Species

About one-fourth of mammal species could disappear from Earth if people don't act now. Animals at places like Smithsonian's National Zoo help us learn more about how to help these animals. The more people learn, the more they can help. People can learn about the types of places that meet animals' needs for food, shelter, and finding mates. That will help people protect the animals' habitats better.

There are many careers that focus on helping protect these animals. You can be a zoologist, a researcher, or a conservationist. You can be a wildlife veterinarian or an animal behaviorist. And there are actions you can take right now. Teach people what you have learned. Open their eyes. Inspire them. And when you get older, ask a zoo how you can volunteer. It takes all of us to save a species.

A marine biologist studies a manatee.

Zoologists feed a tortoise lettuce.

More than 23,000 species of plants and animals are at risk for extinction.

A zoologist hugs a baby orangutan.

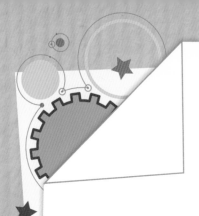

STEAM CHALLENGE

Define the Problem

Smithsonian's National Zoo is always trying to find ways to inspire animals' natural behaviors. One way they do that is by hiding their food in interesting ways. Zoo staff have asked you to design a new puzzle feeder to encourage natural feeding behaviors. They would like a stationary puzzle feeder that can be installed in several animal exhibits.

Constraints: Your design must fit on and fill a poster board that is 60 centimeters × 71 centimeters (22 inches × 28 inches).

Criteria: Your puzzle feeder must have three different challenges for animals to get food. To make sure it is challenging, it should be difficult or impossible for a person to grab small items in the puzzle feeder, such as counters, using just their thumbs and pointer fingers.

Research and Brainstorm

What are some ways that humans are taking action to protect endangered species? How are zoos part of the effort? How do zoos help inspire animals' natural behaviors? What are some ways they hide food for animals?

Design and Build

Sketch your puzzle feeder. Make sure it includes three different puzzles or challenges. What purpose will each part serve? What materials will work best? Build the model.

Test and Improve

Add small items to your puzzle feeder, such as counters or bird feed. Present your design to your friends. Have a team member demonstrate the difficulty of the challenges by trying to grab small items with their thumb and pointer finger. Did it work? How can you improve it? Modify your design and try again.

Reflect and Share

Would you need to modify your design for larger animals to use the puzzle feeder? What other materials could you use? How do you think habitat designers decide what to include in a zoo exhibit?

Glossary

bile—a substance that helps the body digest fats

breed—to mate or produce young plants or animal babies

calories—a unit of heat used to show how much energy foods will produce

carcasses—bodies of dead animals

carnivores—animals that eat meat

conservationists—people who work to protect animals, plants, and natural resources or to prevent the loss or waste of natural resources

dormant—not active but able to become active

endangered—very rare and in danger of dying out completely

evolved—slowly developed or changed into a better, more advanced, or more complex state

extinction—the state of no longer existing

gut bacteria—bacteria in a digestive system that help digest food

lowland—areas where the land is at, near, or below the level of the sea, and where there are not mountains or large hills

mate—an animal that breeds with another animal

omnivores—animals that eat both plants and meat

petitions—documents that people sign to show that they want an organization or a person to change or do something

poachers—people who illegally catch or kill animals

species—groups of animals that are similar and can produce young together

vulnerable—likely to become endangered

wetlands—areas of land that are covered with shallow water

zoologists—people who study animals and animal behavior

Index

CAREER ADVICE
from Smithsonian

Do you want to help save species?
Here are some tips to get you started.

"Breaking into the zoo-keeping field can be challenging. You may want to study science to become a vet. Or you could donate your time to be a volunteer at a zoo. When you are older, try interning at a zoo. That will teach you a lot about what keepers do and how you can help."—*Gwen Cooper and Jordana Todd, Animal Keepers*

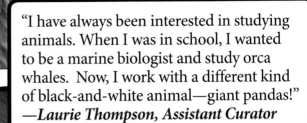

"I have always been interested in studying animals. When I was in school, I wanted to be a marine biologist and study orca whales. Now, I work with a different kind of black-and-white animal—giant pandas!" —*Laurie Thompson, Assistant Curator*